SUPER-CHARGED!

FUNNY CARS

BY

Susan Creighton

PUBLISHED BY

CRESTWOOD HOUSE

New York

CIP

LIBRARY OF CONGRESS CATALOGING IN PUBLICATION DATA

Creighton, Susan.
  Funny cars
  (Super-Charged!)
  Includes index.
  SUMMARY: Describes the sport of funny car racing, an event in drag racing competition,
including its history, types of funny cars, the drag strip, and famous drivers.
  1. Drag racing—United States—Juvenile literature. [1. Drag racing.] I. Title.
GV1029.3.C74   1988   796.7'2—dc19   87-29016
ISBN 0-89686-362-X

International Standard Book Number:	Library of Congress Catalog Card Number:
0-89686-362-X	87-29016

CREDITS

Cover: CJS Racing: (Carol Steimer Bailey)
FPG International: (Phillip Wallick) 12, 24-25
CJS Racing: (Carol Steimer Bailey) 4, 7, 8, 9, 10-11, 13, 14-15, 16, 17, 18-19, 20, 21, 22,
  26-27, 29, 30-31, 32, 34, 35, 36, 37, 38-39, 40, 42-43, 44

CRESTWOOD HOUSE

Macmillan Publishing Company
866 Third Avenue
New York, NY 10022
Collier Macmillan Canada, Inc.

Printed in the United States of America
First Edition
10 9 8 7 6 5 4 3

TABLE OF CONTENTS

A Funny Car headed for action!

FUNNY BUSINESS

Imagine hanging around with a bunch of guys whose nicknames are "The Mongoose," "The Snake," "The Ace," or "Shoe." Sound like a gang you'd want to avoid? Well, maybe not. If you like drag racing—and Funny Cars in particular—then this is the group you'd like to meet. The nicknames belong to a few of Funny Car racing's most famous drivers: Tom McEwen, Don Prudhomme, Ed McCulloch, and Don Schumacher.

Funny Car racing is one of the most exciting events in drag racing competition. The colorful cars—and their even more colorful drivers—make it a unique speed sport that has grown in popularity since the mid-1960's. But to fully appreciate Funny Cars, a fan needs to know a little of the history of drag racing.

THE FASTEST SPORT AROUND

Drag racing takes only seconds of the participants' time, covers a quarter-mile (2/5 of a kilometer) of track, and is probably the fastest-growing spectator sport in the United States.

After World War II, American servicemen returned home to their families. By the late 1940's, owning a car had become a common goal for most of them. As these young men bought and drove their cars, they developed a strong interest in working on their own engines. Making the cars run faster and better became a hobby with them.

Soon, street racing (or "hot rodding" as it was later called) began on side roads and on abandoned airstrips. At first, these races were just for fun. There were few rules, and almost anyone could join in. A man named Wally Parks of southern California organized some early speed trials. With his guidance, the backroad races became the sport of "drag racing" that we know today.

Wally Parks was the first editor of *Hot Rod Magazine,* which became a popular magazine for racing fans. Before long, Parks set up the National Hot Rod Association (NHRA). This organization created the rules for racing. Parks' organization helped hot rod clubs all over the country set up and supervise drag racing events.

In 1955, Parks and the NHRA staged the first national championship drag race on an abandoned airfield in Great Bend, Kansas. The only prizes the winners took home that year were trophies, but something great had been started. The hobby of hot rodding had "grown up" into the sport of drag racing.

As drag racing's popularity spread throughout the country, many technical experts were drawn into the contests. Cars which originally were nothing more than stripped-down versions of street automobiles

Colorful cars and even more colorful drivers have increased Funny Cars' popularity.

began to be changed. Engines were beefed up. Special fuel mixtures were made. Rear tires got bigger and wider. A lot of experimenting went on.

The experts were making the cars accelerate (speed up) quicker, reaching faster top speeds. In 1955, the best elapsed time recorded at Great Bend, Kansas, was by a driver named Calvin Rice. His car, a Mercury dragster, covered the quarter-mile distance in 10.30 seconds. His speed as he crossed the finish line was clocked at 143.95 miles per hour (mph) or 231 kilometers per hour (km/h). By 1986, a driver named Darrell Gwynn would cut that 1955 record elapsed time in half to 5.261 seconds and practically double the top speed to 278.55 mph (448 Km/h)!

FROM BACK ROADS TO BIG BUSINESS

Although drag racing in the early years was organized to give amateurs a safe way to enjoy their hobby, things have recently taken a different turn.

A Funny Car shows off its oversized rear wheels.

Today, a large corporation may "own" a racing car and employ a professional to drive its car to victory. Sponsors pump a great deal of money into drag racing today. It's now big business. Auto parts suppliers, shoe manufacturers, beverage companies, and even the Boy Scouts have had their decals on a race car.

But drag racing always has room for the amateurs. Although the professional categories attract the most attention, the amateur meets are extremely popular with the fans. Many local men and women have captured the limelight in an amateur event.

Drivers decorate their Funny Cars with their sponsor's name.

Because Funny Car racing is expensive, it has become big business.

11

A Funny Car dragster.

PROFESSIONAL DRAG RACING TODAY

The number of professional categories in drag racing is usually limited to three. The NHRA recognizes Top Fuel dragsters (TF), nitromethane-fueled Funny Cars (FC), and Pro Stock (PRO). Two smaller governing bodies which also oversee drag racing events are the American Hot Rod Association (AHRA) and the International Hot Rod Association (IHRA). Their categories are somewhat different, but everybody has a Funny Car category! These vehicles have definitely become a favorite with drag racing fans.

Funny Cars have been around a long time. Back in the early '60's, changes in wheelbase and weight distribution were made to increase a car's speed. When the steel bodies were put back in place, they didn't fit quite right over the new oversized rear wheels. This made the cars look, well, "funny." And so the name Funny Cars was coined. Although the Funny Cars of today don't look much like their

It takes hours to prepare Funny Cars for a race.

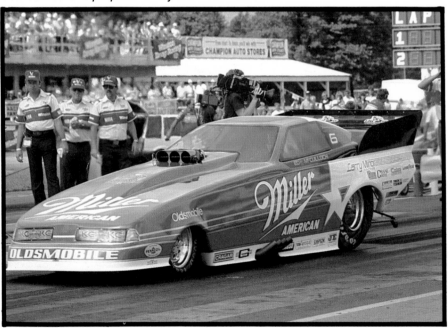

A flopper's body is only a lightweight shell.

relatives of 20 years ago, the name has stuck.

In professional drag racing, speed and elapsed time records are set by drivers whose cars have maximum horsepower and minimum weight. That has always meant the Top Fuel category. But Funny

Cars are not much more than Top Fuel dragsters with a lightweight "shell" draped over them. These "floppers" (as they are affectionately called) are the second fastest cars in drag racing. The Pro Stock category follows, with much lower top speeds.

A super-charged V-8 engine provides the power for a Funny Car.

WHAT MAKES
A FUNNY CAR?

The drag racing rulebook defines Funny Cars carefully. They must be self-starting, with an aluminum supercharged V-8 engine not larger than 500 cubic inches (8,193 cubic centimeters). The wheelbase must be between 100 and 125 inches (254 and 317 centimeters). Maximum rear tire size is 17

A spoiler directs airflow and helps increase a Funny Car's speed.

inches (43 centimeters) wide, 114 inches (289 centimeters) in circumference (the distance around the tire). There are many regulations limiting the design of the body and size of the rear spoiler. The spoiler is a flat piece of metal mounted on the front or back of a car. It directs the airflow and improves the Funny Car's speed. The body of a Funny Car is made of fiberglass or carbon fiber, and weighs just over 200 pounds (90 kilograms). Car and driver

A driver strapped securely into his car.

together must not weigh more than 2,050 pounds (930 kilograms).

The "floppy" body of the Funny Car is its most distinctive feature. It is a one-piece, molded shell. The entire body is lifted off the chassis, or frame of the car, to allow the driver to get in and out.

Some of the most frightening and heart-stopping moments in racing history have occurred when a

Funny Car's shell has melted during a race. This has often meant obscured vision for the driver, whose ability is tested to the limit.

There is always the chance of a serious accident in drag racing. The governing organizations insist on strict safety rules. But nothing is foolproof. Drivers must be strapped into their cars. They must wear fireproof protective clothing from head to foot,

Two Funny Cars ready for the final countdown.

including a crash helmet and gloves.

Funny Cars have their engines up front, so they must have a fire wall between the engine and the driver and an emergency escape hatch in the roof. The transmission must also have a protective shield to prevent any moving parts from striking the driver should it come apart.

Although Funny Cars must have four-wheel disc brakes, dual rear parachutes are also required. The

To ensure safety, drivers wear fireproof clothing from head to toe.

The body of a Funny Car can be changed at any time.

parachutes work harder than the brakes to bring the car to a stop.

Funny Cars have had all kinds of body styles over the years—Fords, Chevys, Plymouths, and Buicks, to name only a few. And a racer's car is often painted with fiery colors and designs so spectators will recognize their favorite Funny Car driver. The variety is one reason why Funny Cars are so popular. The bodies are like a snake's skin. When they are damaged or burned, they are removed and thrown away. Some drivers have been known to buy "spare" bodies from other racers in the middle of an event just to stay in the race!

THE FUEL

To make cars perform better, the Funny Car drivers and their crews have modified their engines, their wheelbases and tires, and their bodies. The question, then, is what do they feed these cars to make them move so fast?

The answer: a mixture of nitromethane (93-95%) and alcohol. Nitromethane—used many years ago as a rocket fuel—makes a bigger "explosion" than gasoline inside a car's engine. This means more power. The average automobile weighs several thousand pounds and is driven by a 150-horsepower engine. A record-setting Funny Car is totally different. It weighs less than 2,000 pounds (900 kilograms) and generates over 3,000 horsepower.

This power can accelerate a Funny Car to 100 mph (160 Km/h) in just over one second. And it can reach a top speed of more than 270 mph (430 Km/h) in about 5½ seconds! But nitromethane is not cheap. It costs about $30.00 per gallon. And a Funny Car in top form will use eight gallons in a single run. That's $240 for six seconds of driving.

Funny Cars burn modified rocket fuel.

A driver spins his rear tires in the burnout area.

THE DRAG STRIP

The regulation drag strip is 1,320 feet (400 meters) long, or exactly one quarter-mile (²/₅ of a kilometer). It is a straight line, unlike most other racing arenas which are oval.

Before the cars approach the staging area, or starting line, the drivers will do wet and dry "burnouts" in the burnout area. A burnout is the spinning of the rear tires to heat them up. Driving through a little water first (wet burnout) helps clean the tires for better traction. A dry burnout creates heat in both the tires and the clutch. That makes for a good take-off from the starting line.

A car with a warm engine performs better than one that's cooled. Each driver keeps his engine running as he waits for the signal to race.

At the far end of the track the drivers will cross the finish line at top speed. Their speeds will be recorded electronically, and their elapsed times will be measured. Then the drivers will activate their brakes and parachutes as they move into the shutdown area.

THE LIGHTS

A lot has changed since Wally Parks' time. The flagman who signalled the start of each race has been replaced by the "Christmas Tree" starting system. Lights signal the countdown for each driver. No flagman is needed. The "tree" makes sure drivers start at the same position and at the same time. It is located on the center line of the track 20 feet (6 meters) in front of the starting line. The sequence for races in all professional categories (Top Fuel, Funny Car, and Pro Stock) is the same.

First, the top orange Pre-Staged lights warn drivers that they are within moments of being "staged" to race. Next, the Staged lights flash on when the vehicles' front wheels break the electronic light beam. The cars are now at exactly the same position.

The orange Countdown lights flash the "get ready" signal. Four-tenths of a second later, the green Start lights signal "GO!" Both cars take off at the same time.

The red Foul Start lights will flash if a car breaks the light beam before the green has been lit. The Foul Start lights disqualify the driver who has triggered them.

The "Christmas Tree" signals the drivers that the race is about to begin.

A crew member signals the driver that his car is ready.

Drivers keep their best elapsed times in a series of time trials.

ELIMINATIONS

Most drag racing events in the professional categories start with a field of 16 positions. But there may be as many as 50 contestants trying to win those 16 spots! Before the positions can be given to any drivers, all drivers must compete in a series of time trials. Each driver keeps his best elapsed time for the series. The 16 drivers with the lowest elapsed times are awarded the starting positions.

Sixteen races are held to get eight winners. The eight winners then move into the quarter-final eliminations. The four winners of the quarter-finals move into the semi-finals. The two winners of the semi-finals meet each other in the final round of the competition. The winner of that round is declared the overall winner.

POINTS AND CHAMPIONSHIPS

All three drag racing associations (NHRA, IHRA, and AHRA) hold competitions throughout the year. Drivers may compete in these events if they are members of the sponsoring association. Drag racing is expensive and time-consuming, so most racers only compete in one association's events. But some racers have the time and money to enter competitions in more than one association.

Each of the three associations award points for winning an event. Every driver who qualifies for one of the 16 starting positions will win some points. The better a driver does in an event, the more points he will earn.

At the end of the racing season (usually in November), each association awards a bonus to the driver who accumulated the most points during that year.

Experienced crew members are an important factor for a winning team.

HOW DO YOU WIN A FUNNY CAR RACE?

Winning is a combination of several things: having a state-of-the-art dragster; the right fuel mixture; a lightweight, aerodynamic body that won't buckle at high speeds; a crew that can anticipate problems and correct them before they happen; a driver who is

The driver is the "living part" of the race car.

a "living part" of the car; and a sponsor or group of sponsors willing to support the cost of this team effort.

There is another key to winning a drag race, however. In oval track and road races, pacing is important. Each lap gives a driver the chance to make up lost time. In drag racing, however, there are only about six seconds of race. *Everything* depends

Funny Car bodies are tested in wind tunnels before they hit the race track.

on how quickly and cleanly the driver leaves the starting line on the green light. Many races have been lost at the starting line.

The reflexes and reaction time of the driver are just as important as the car's ability to respond. There are many new technologies to improve the car's performance. Wind-tunnel testing has become common for body design. Most cars are now computer-equipped for solving engine problems, and more advances are made each year. But for the driver, there is no substitute for experience and love of racing. These key ingredients can't be bought at an auto parts store!

IS THERE ANY MONEY IN RACING?

Ten years ago, money was a serious problem in drag racing. The costs of maintaining and upgrading a car, repairing it after an engine blowout, and

Since drag racing is hard on the cars, they need constant maintenance.

Funny Car racers work hard to put on a good show for the spectators.

traveling the racing circuit made many drivers quit. The prize money at most competitive events was not enough to cover the most basic expenses of the drivers.

Fortunately, time is changing all that. Drag racing has become a popular attraction on television as well

as at the local drag strip. Companies have begun making large contributions to improve racing sites. Cash awards to drivers are on the rise.

The NHRA announced a record bonus fund of $771,500 for 1987. The Top Fuel and Funny Car champions will each receive $100,000 and the Pro

Don "The Snake" Prudhomme in his Skoal-sponsored Funny Car.

Stock winner will get $50,000 from the new point fund. A bonus fund for all professional drivers has also been created. Professional drivers will be paid $250 to $500 for each round of competition they win during the season. Runners-up and third-place finishers will also receive bonuses ranging between $5,000 and $15,000 per driver.

As some drivers have said, "Better late than never!"

THE PEOPLE IN FUNNY CAR RACING

Since 1969, when Funny Cars first became an official category in the NHRA, Funny Cars have earned a well-deserved spot in the professional racing history book. But racing is not just about cars. It's about the people who drive them, too.

No book would be complete without mentioning the names of some of Funny Cars' most famous people.

Don "The Snake" Prudhomme has been racing professionally since 1962. He started in Top Fuel. After winning many national events and five career Top Fuel titles, he turned to Funny Car racing in 1974. He is the top Funny Car winner in NHRA history with 35 national event victories and four World Championship titles.

Drag racing attracts thousands of fans each season.

Three consecutive World Funny Car Championships in the NHRA and two World Funny Car titles in the IHRA put Ray Beadle at the head of the class. He has an impressive collection of national event victories in both NHRA and IHRA competitions.

Frank Hawley is a two-time winner of the NHRA Winston Funny Car Championship. He now teaches the finer points of Funny Car racing at his own drag racing school in Gainesville, Florida.

The 1987 NHRA Funny Car champ (he has two world championships in the NHRA and one in the IHRA), Kenny Bernstein has traded his Ford Tempo car body for a Buick LeSabre body this year. In

addition to his many national championships, Kenny
has set Funny Car speed and elapsed time records
(271.41 mph/436 Km/h; 5.425 elapsed time in
different events). He was the first, with crew chief
Dale Armstrong, to use the Lockheed Wind Tunnel
in Marietta, Georgia, to help design his car body.
Kenny also brought on-board computers into the
world of drag racing with his Racepak Computer.

All Funny Car drivers work hard to improve their
cars. They want to put on a good show for the
crowd—and be the best racer. Although their cars
might look strange, the drivers know their racers
have a lot of power. Funny Car Racing is fast and
exciting—every time!

A Funny Car driver mentally prepares for the next big race.

FOR MORE INFORMATION

For more information about drag racing in general or Funny Car racing in particular, contact:

THE NATIONAL HOT ROD ASSOCIATION
2035 Financial Way
P.O. Box 5555
Glendora, CA 91740

THE INTERNATIONAL HOT ROD
ASSOCIATION
P.O. Box 3029
Bristol, TN 37625

THE AMERICAN HOT ROD ASSOCIATION
111 North Hayford Road
Spokane, WA 99204

GLOSSARY/INDEX

ACCELERATE 7, 23 — *To increase the speed of a vehicle.*

BURNOUT 27 — *The process of heating up the tires of a car by spinning its wheels. A burnout is important before a race because it provides better traction for the car.*

CHASSIS 18 — *The framework that supports the body and engine of a vehicle.*

COUNTDOWN LIGHTS 28, 29 — *Commonly known as the "Christmas Tree", this set of lights flashes in sequence before a race, preparing racers for the final flash of the Go! light. Also, the Countdown lights ensure that all drivers start at the same time and from the same point.*

ELAPSED TIME 7, 14, 28, 32, 43 — *The amount of time it takes to race from the start to the finish line.*

FIRE WALL 20 — *A fireproof divider between the driver and the engine.*

FLOPPERS 15, 18 — *A dragster with a lightweight shell over its whole body. Another term for Funny Car.*

HORSEPOWER 14, 23 — *The unit for measuring the power of an engine.*

NITROMETHANE 12, 23 — *An old type of rocket fuel that is mixed with alcohol and used to give Funny Cars their extraordinary power and speed.*

46

GLOSSARY/INDEX

SPOILER 17 — *A flat piece of metal mounted on the front or back of a car. When a car is racing, the spoiler directs the airflow around it to prevent lift and improve the car's speed.*

SPONSOR 8, 35 — *A person or company that gives a race car driver money, tools, and equipment. The driver decorates his car with the sponsors' name and product.*

STAGING AREA 27 — *A small part of the race track located right behind the starting line. Right before they race, drivers warm up their cars at the staging area.*

TRACTION 27 — *Preventing a wheel from slipping and sliding on a road or race track surface.*

WHEELBASE 13, 16, 23 — *The distance between the front and rear axle in a vehicle.*